With special thanks to Dr. Sylvia Hope, California Academy of Sciences, for her review and suggestions, which were so helpful in creating and completing this book.

Parent's Introduction

We Both Read is the first series of books designed to invite parents and children to share the reading of a story by taking turns reading aloud. This "shared reading" innovation, which was developed with reading education specialists, invites parents to read the more complex text and storyline on the left-hand pages. Then, children can be encouraged to read the right-hand pages, which feature less complex text and storyline, specifically written for the beginning reader.

Reading aloud is one of the most important activities parents can share with their child to assist them in their reading development. However, *We Both Read* goes beyond reading *to* a child and allows parents to share the reading *with* a child. *We Both Read* is so powerful and effective because it combines two key elements in learning: "modeling" (the parent reads) and "doing" (the child reads). The result is not only faster reading development for the child, but a much more enjoyable and enriching experience for both!

You may find it helpful to read the entire book aloud yourself the first time, then invite your child to participate in the second reading. In some books, a few more difficult words will first be introduced in the parent's text, distinguished with **bold lettering**. Pointing out, and even discussing, these words will help familiarize your child with them and help to build your child's vocabulary. Also, note that a "talking parent" icon ⊚⊃ precedes the parent's text and a "talking child" icon ⊂⊚ precedes the child's text.

We encourage you to share and interact with your child as you read the book together. If your child is having difficulty, you might want to mention a few things to help them. "Sounding out" is good, but it will not work with all words. Children can pick up clues about the words they are reading from the story, the context of the sentence, or even the pictures. Some stories have rhyming patterns that might help. It might also help them to touch the words with their finger as they read, to better connect the voice sound and the printed word.

Sharing the *We Both Read* books together will engage you and your child in an interactive adventure in reading! It is a fun and easy way to encourage and help your child to read—and a wonderful way to start them off on a lifetime of reading enjoyment!

We Both Read: Animals Under Our Feet

_____

Text Copyright © 2007 by Sindy McKay.
Illustrations Copyright © 2007 by Judith Hunt.
Use of photographs provided by: Brand X, California Academy of Sciences,
Corbis, Corel, Creatas, Digital Vision, Image 100, Imagestate & Photodisc.
Page 10 (cicada): Gladys Lucille Smith © California Academy of Sciences.
Page 15 (groundhog): Dr. Lloyd Glenn Ingles © California Academy of Sciences.
Page 23 (badger): Gerald & Buff Corsi © California Academy of Sciences.

We Both Read® is a trademark of Treasure Bay, Inc.

Published by
Treasure Bay, Inc.
P.O. Box 119
Novato, CA 94948 USA

PRINTED IN SINGAPORE

Library of Congress Catalog Card Number: 2006932224

Hardcover ISBN-10: 1-60115-003-2
Hardcover ISBN-13: 978-1-60115-003-5
Paperback ISBN-10: 1-60115-004-0
Paperback ISBN-13: 978-1-60115-004-2

We Both Read® Books
Patent No. 5,957,693

Visit us online at:
www.webothread.com

Animals
Under Our Feet

By Sindy McKay

Illustrations by Judith Hunt

TREASURE BAY

salamander

cicada

meadow mole

Have you ever walked on top of someone's home? You probably have! Many **animals** make their homes underground and we may not even know they are there.

earthworm

mole

ant

What **animals** do you see?

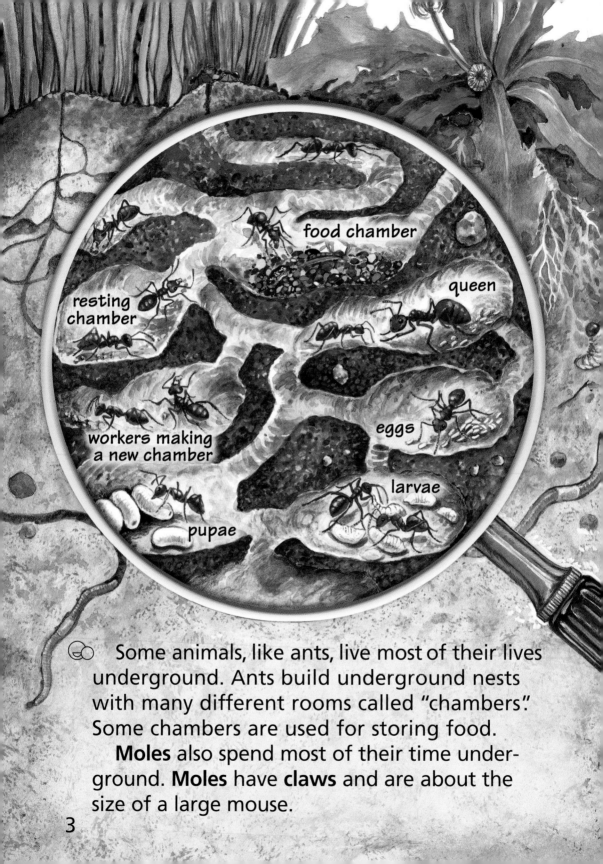

food chamber

queen

resting
chamber

workers making
a new chamber

eggs

larvae

pupae

Some animals, like ants, live most of their lives
underground. Ants build underground nests
with many different rooms called "chambers."
Some chambers are used for storing food.
Moles also spend most of their time underground. **Moles** have **claws** and are about the
size of a large mouse.

 **Moles** have small eyes, but they have big strong **claws**.

They can use their **claws** to dig very fast.

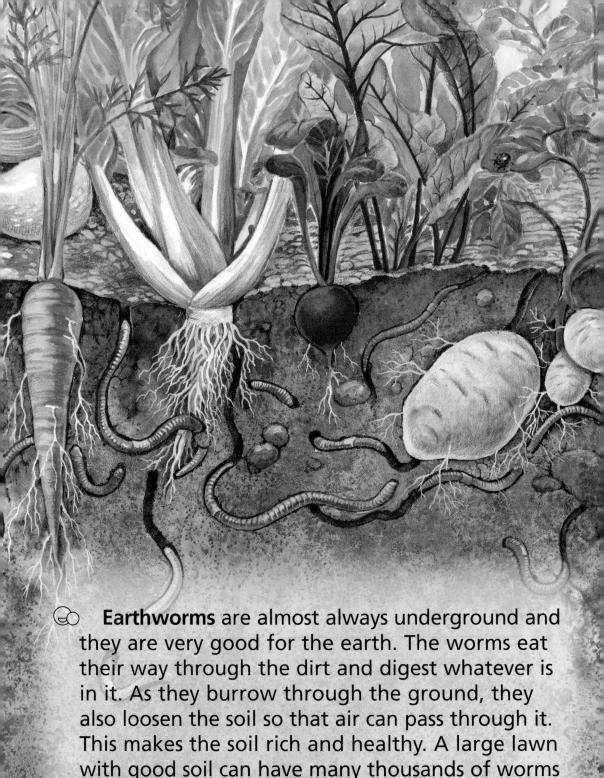

Earthworms are almost always underground and they are very good for the earth. The worms eat their way through the dirt and digest whatever is in it. As they burrow through the ground, they also loosen the soil so that air can pass through it. This makes the soil rich and healthy. A large lawn with good soil can have many thousands of worms in it!

5

Earthworms may not be pretty, but they are very good for the plants and trees.

Meerkats spend some time below ground and some time above ground. They live in large groups called "mobs". One meerkat stands watch to warn the others when danger approaches, then they all run into their underground burrows.

 **Meerkats** can stand on their back legs. They use their tail like another leg.

adult
cicada

laying eggs
in tree branch

nymph

molting
adult

mature
nymph

nymph
(feeding on roots)

The **cicada** is an insect that lives part of its life cycle underground and part of it above ground.
A periodical **cicada** starts as an egg. When the egg hatches into a nymph, it burrows into the soil near a tree root where it feeds on the tree's sap for up to seventeen years!

The cicada on the left is shedding its old skin, a process called molting.

👓 All of the **cicadas** come up out of the ground at the same time.

They sing **cicada** songs. This can be very loud!

10

There are many reasons animals live underground. One very good reason is to be safe
from predators.

Black-tailed prairie dogs live in large groups
called "towns". The towns have a complex system
of connecting burrows underground. The "dogs"
retreat into these burrows when threatened.

Prairie dogs can make a sound like a **whistle**.

If a "dog" **whistles**, the whole "town" may go underground to be safe.

   **Prairie** dogs are social animals with a sophisticated natural animal language. They make unique sounds to warn each other of the presence of different predators, such as hawks, owls, eagles, coyotes, and badgers.

 **Prairie** dogs are not really dogs, but they can bark. When they bark, they sound a lot like a dog.

 **Groundhogs** are also hunted by many animals, including wolves, coyotes, bobcats, and foxes. They move very slowly, so they can't run away from these predators. The best they can do is to go underground into their burrows for protection.

Do you know about **Groundhog** Day?

Groundhog Day is the only holiday named for an animal.

Another reason some animals live underground is to protect themselves from heat or cold.

The **desert tortoise** of the Mojave Desert lives where the temperatures range from 140 degrees Fahrenheit to well below freezing. It spends much of its life burrowed safely under the sand to protect itself from getting too hot or too cold.

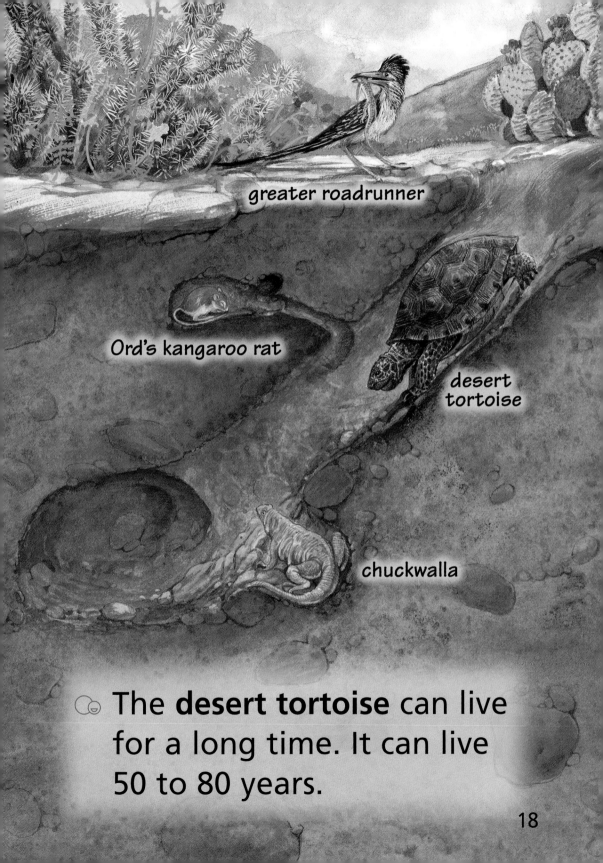

greater roadrunner

Ord's kangaroo rat

desert tortoise

chuckwalla

The **desert tortoise** can live for a long time. It can live 50 to 80 years.

 Burrows and dens come in handy for animals that hibernate. Some animals hibernate all **winter** long. They go into a deep sleep where their body temperature drops and their heart beats very slowly.

Other animals go to sleep during the **winter** for days or weeks. They wake up to drink water and eat food. Then they go back to sleep again.

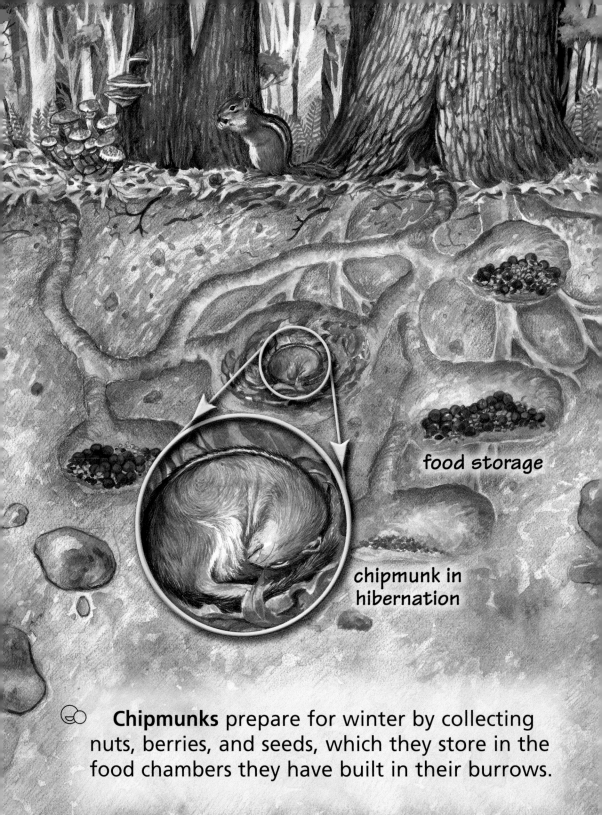

food storage

chipmunk in
hibernation

Chipmunks prepare for winter by collecting
nuts, berries, and seeds, which they store in the
food chambers they have built in their burrows.

 **Chipmunks** can carry nuts and seeds in their cheeks.

Many burrowing animals look underground for food, such as bulbs, roots, worms, grubs, and insects. **Badgers** especially love to burrow for these kinds of food.

Sometimes animals must **fight** to protect themselves.

Badgers do not look for a **fight**, but they will **fight** if they have to.

 **Armadillos** have large claws that help them dig into the earth in search of food. They also have long tongues to help them slurp up ants, beetles, and worms.

sidewinder rattlesnake

nine-banded armadillo

Armadillos dig many dens. Other animals move in when the **armadillos** leave.

One animal that may move into an abandoned armadillo den is the **burrowing owl**. It will also take over the abandoned burrows and dens of badgers, ground squirrels, gophers, or foxes.

The **burrowing owl** can also dig out a new home of its own in the ground.

American bison

black-footed ferret

prairie dogs

    Ferrets rarely dig their own burrows. Instead, they usually move into other animals' burrows, including prairie dog burrows. **Ferrets** are long and skinny so they can get down the narrow holes. **Ferrets** are meat-eaters, so they may simply drive the prairie dogs out—or eat them for dinner!

 **Ferrets** hunt at night.
They hunt for mice
and other animals.

Dens and burrows are relatively safe places where many animals go to have their babies and raise their young.

Foxes and coyotes often dig their own dens, but sometimes they use the abandoned burrows of other animals.

Baby foxes love to play.
They are very cute!

Some **rabbits** raise their babies in burrows which they dig with their powerful hind legs. Baby bunny **rabbits** are born blind and without fur, so burrows are especially important to keep them safe and warm.

 **Rabbits** like to be with other **rabbits**. Many **rabbits** stay together like a family.

Jackrabbits are close cousins of "bunny" rabbits, but they have longer back legs and can leap farther into the air. Baby jackrabbits are born with their eyes open and with lots of fur, so they don't need as much protection as baby bunnies do.

Some kinds of rabbits make very good pets.

The ground below is truly an amazing resource. Many animals live beneath it. Plants and trees grow out of it. And even more animals live on top of it.

 We live on top of it too.

   So think about it the next time you go running across a lawn or walking through the woods or skipping across a meadow. You just may be stepping on top of someone's home!

beetle

mouse

garter snake

mole

earthworm

shrew

rabbit

groundhog

It's okay. They don't mind it at all.

If you liked
Animals Under Our Feet, here are two other
We Both Read® Books you are sure to enjoy!

Featuring delightful photographs, this book explores the wonderful world of both popular and unusual pets. In simple language, it discusses the joys, as well as the responsibilities, of pet ownership. This book is sure to be a hit with everyone who has, or even wishes they could have, a pet.

To see all the We Both Read books that are available,
just go online to **www.webothread.com**

This simple Level 1 book explores the seasons through
the changing weather and the changing activities of
both children and animals. There is a brief description
of why the earth has four seasons, but most of the
book is devoted to the delightful new world that each
season brings into our life.